Grimsoning The Eagle's Claw

Grimsoning
the Eagle's Claw

THE VIKING POEMS OF
RǪGNVALDR KALI KOLSSON
EARL OF ORKNEY

Translated & introduced
by Ian Crockatt
with a preface by Kevin Crossley-Holland

PUBLICATIONS
2014

Published by Arc Publications,
Nanholme Mill, Shaw Wood Road
Todmorden OL14 6DA, UK
www.arcpublications.co.uk

Translation & Introduction copyright © Ian Crockatt, 2014
Preface copyright © Kevin Crossley-Holland, 2014

Design by Tony Ward & Ben Styles
Printed in Great Britain by
TJ International, Padstow, Cornwall

978 1908376 60 2 (pbk)
978 1908376 61 9 (hbk)
978 1908376 62 6 (ebk)

Cover image and illustrations by Wenna Crockatt

Arc Classics:
New Translations of Great Poets of the Past
Series Editor: Jean Boase-Beier

Contents

Preface

Not a storm-surge, not yet, but the tide of scholarly and popular interest in Viking culture has never flowed more strongly. One has only to glance at a recent bibliography to see the welter of papers, histories, critical studies and translations to have appeared since the turn of the century, while the market-place has been flooded by adult, children's and graphic novels, films, cartoons and computer games, and intellectual enquiry and general appeal have come together in the major exhibition, *Vikings: life and legend*, at the British Museum in early 2014.

But although more than five thousand skaldic poems composed between the ninth and thirteenth centuries survive, they have been sideswept not only because they are so very dense and allusive, and packed with kennings, but because translators have baulked at the poems' extremely demanding verse form.

In his exemplary introduction, Ian Crockatt describes the classic skaldic stanza, the *dróttkvætt*, as exoskeletal, in which the form necessarily (if only scarcely) contains the contents, and makes his point with a memorable comparison – but I won't steal his thunder! Crockatt then convincingly argues that a translation can only be successful if it 'seeks equivalents for the original's sound-patterns and imaginative reach as well as its narrative sense.' William Morris was the last published translator to attempt this, one hundred and fifty years ago.

So it's wonderful to report that the forty-one skaldic verses in *Crimsoning the Eagle's Claw*, most of them preserved in *Orkneyinga Saga*, are really fine translations of fine poems. When I first read a few of them several years ago, I noted how passionate they were, how they had got under my skin, and were waking me up in the middle of the night. In this short preface, I would just add that the best of them are akin to fierce sparklers, momentarily lighting the dark; they're like random jottings and observations; spirited, almost gamey, and marvellously skilful.

What I (and I certainly won't be alone) find immensely exciting is that in these aristocratic, vivid, sensuous poems, I'm meeting a Viking face to face, and of course this gives the book both coherence and thrilling immediacy. Here's the Norwegian who was an Earl of Orkney; the man who founded the beautiful pink cathedral in Kirkwall to house the remains of his martyred uncle, Magnus. Here's a member of the Varangian Guard in Byzantium with stories of the old gods seething in his blood, who was canonised as a Christian saint. A sensitive extrovert... daring yet tender... a lover, a pilgrim, a warrior, a wit: Rǫgnvaldr was all these, and 'bragging' of his own skills, he concludes: 'Best of all, I've mastered / harp-play and poetry .'

A number of Viking poets came from Norway to Orkney, among them Turf-Einar Rognvaldsson ('I can promise you the greatest favour you could wish for', he told his father, 'and that's never to see me again!') and the anonymous skald who composed the *Darraðarljóð*, the spear-song sung by the Valkyries after the Battle of Clontarf in 1014, and the author of *Orkneyinga Saga*. And as one might expect, their work and Rǫgnvaldr's poems bear the stamp of the Northern Isles (just look at Crockatt's notes!) no less than fine but little known Orkney writers such as Samuel Laing and Robert Rendall, and the islands' three important twentieth century writers, Edwin Muir, Eric Linklater and George Mackay Brown. Indeed, they're all part of one thriving cultural story.

Rǫgnvaldr's poems give us precious glimpses of a life lived to the full. They are spirited and generous. They're celebrations. And they are manly.

In a charming *dróttkvætt* of his own by way of envoi, Ian Crockatt makes a promise to Rǫgnvaldr. His superb translations ensure that it is very likely to come true.

Kevin Crossley-Holland

Translator's Introduction

SKALDIC POETRY AND ICELANDIC SAGAS

Rǫgnvaldr jarl Kali Kolsson was a twelfth century Christian Viking, Norwegian by birth and upbringing, and he became joint Earl of Orkney in 1135 at a time when Shetland, and also Caithness on the Scottish mainland, were part of the earldom. He was nephew of St. Magnús, who had previously had a share in the earldom, and Rǫgnvaldr is primarily remembered as the founder of St. Magnus Cathedral in Kirkwall. His uncle's remains were translated there from their initial resting place on Birsay, and his own remains were interred in the cathedral too. Both men died violent deaths and both were later declared saints.

The life of a Viking earl was full of incident – as well as a ruler and warrior Rǫgnvaldr was a law-maker and crusader. He was also a pirate and plunderer, a lover, a scholar and a highly skilled poet. He was popular, accomplished and urbane, a Renaissance man two hundred years before the Renaissance. We know this because his exploits are recorded in *Orkneyinga Saga, The History of the Earls of Orkney,* one of the many sagas written in the Old Norse vernacular during the great flowering of fictional, historical and scholarly texts produced in thirteenth and fourteenth century Iceland.

The sagas frequently contained, or indeed based their narratives round, the intricate and muscular poetry of the skalds, court poets who composed poems in praise of kings and earls in exchange for treasure and patronage. They also covered a wide range of other subject matter in their verse – war, sailing and women were favourites – and were never slow to boast about their own prowess as purveyors of 'Odin's mead', as poetry was frequently called. The very words 'Odin's mead' give an indication of the powers attributed to words and poetry in early medieval Scandinavia. The idea of poetry as a god-given intoxicant which granted those who drank it both wisdom and the power to make poetry, is central to the Old Norse myth of poetry's origins. Skalds, who frequently boasted of their own skills, would have taken great satisfaction in the part which features Odin in the form of an eagle, its crop full of the precious mead ready to be disgorged into cauldrons within the walls of Asgard for the sole use of the gods – and of men especially talented in making verses – having first defecated a smattering outside the walls for poetasters.

Skaldic poetry flourished from the ninth to the thirteenth centuries, and one reason for its inclusion in the sagas was as a means of authenticating the tales and histories they told. The saga-writers believed that ancient, orally-composed verses, passed down through the generations in a highly elaborate, unchanging form and incorporating many sensational images known as 'kennings' (discussed on p. 16), would have been easily remembered and passed on relatively unchanged. The verses were intended to lend the sagas authenticity since they were (allegedly) composed at the time of the actions the prose described, and were therefore likely to be true accounts of real incidents.

By Rǫgnvaldr's time making skaldic poems had become one of the skills of a fully-rounded aristocrat, and it was not unusual for kings and earls themselves to compose verse. *Orkneyinga Saga* is particularly rich in poetry because as well as gathering skalds round him at court, Rǫgnvaldr was prolific as a poet himself.

VERSE-FORM

Skaldic poetry is notorious for the complexity of its verse-form which, since it was composed orally, was defined entirely by its sound patterns and rhythms. Poetry preserved in the sagas was written down like prose and is often visually indistinguishable from the text around it. Each classic skaldic stanza, known as *dróttkvætt,* is composed of a system of eight six-syllable lines with preset patterns of stress, alliteration, internal rhyme, half-rhyme and trochaic line-endings. *Dróttkvætt* means 'verse suitable for reciting before the court' and all except one of Rǫgnvaldr's poems (*'They sail to Byzantium',* p. 78) are composed in this strict form. An example is given below, with the alliteration and internal rhyme and half-rhyme schemes indicated by bold letters and underlining respectively. The approximations of the translated poem are evident.

> **Vé**r hǫfum **v**aðnar <u>leir</u>ur
> vikur **fimm** me**g**in<u>grimm</u>ar;
> <u>saur</u>s **v**asa **v**ant, es **v**ǫ́<u>r</u>um,
> **v**iðr, í Grímsbœ <u>mið</u>jum.
> <u>Nús</u>, þats **m**ǫ́<u>s</u> of **m**ýrar
> **m**egin<u>kát</u>liga <u>lǫ́t</u>um
> **b**randa <u>elg</u> á <u>**b**ylg</u>jur
> **Bj**ǫr<u>gyn</u>jar til <u>dyn</u>ja.

> **M**uck, slime, **m**ud. We <u>wad</u>ed
> for five **m**ired <u>week</u>s, <u>reek</u>ing,
> silt-<u>foul</u>ed **b**ilge-**b**oards <u>sour</u>ing
> in <u>Grim</u>sby **b**ay. <u>Nim</u>bly

now, our **p**roud-**p**ro<u>w</u>ed, Bergen-
bound Sea-Elk **p**ound<u>s</u> over
<u>wave</u>-paved <u>a</u>u<u>k</u>-moors, <u>lock</u>s **h**orns
with <u>foam</u>-crests, **b**ows <u>b</u>oo<u>m</u>ing.

Briefly, it should be noted that each stanza's eight
lines is made up of two sets of four – a few of the
poems are only four lines long – and each six-syllable line ends with a trochee, that is a stressed syllable followed by an unstressed syllable. The last
syllable is always unrhymed, and the internal half-
rhymes and rhymes are on syllables, not necessarily whole words. Full rhymes occur in even lines,
half-rhymes in odd lines. The alliterative pattern,
which ties the lines together in twos, means odd
lines have two alliterating syllables, and the first
stressed syllable of the following even line alliter-
ates with them. So in the Old Norse poem above
the 'v's of *vér* and *vaðnar* in line one alliterate with
the 'v' of *vikur* in line two. These basic rules are
complicated by unpredictable word order which
means it is not always obvious which word relates
to which unless the reader has a full grasp of Old
Norse grammar. A further complication is the
skalds' frequent use of 'intercalation', a technique
in which a sentence is interrupted by a phrase, or
another sentence, and then continued, the effect
being to both slow down the rhythm and to insert

15

more information in the building up of a picture or situation. The poem '*His first encounter with monks, on Westray*' (p. 32) has one example of intercalation in the Old Norse, and I have used two in the translation.

The overall effect of this accumulation of apparently inflexible rules is that each poem becomes a highly tensioned allusive artefact, the best of which achieve vivid, transformative effects and feeling, while the not-so-good have been likened to crossword puzzles requiring antiquated specialist knowledge few aspire to. Combined with the fact that Old Norse is a dead language, and that Northern European mythology and culture have for centuries been overshadowed in Europe by Greek and Roman classicism, it is no wonder that this poetry, a genuinely unique treasure – and in Rǫgnvaldr's case a marvellous contribution to poetic achievement in Scotland – is almost unknown.

KENNINGS

Kennings are circumlocutions, which have metaphorical features, and are usually comprised of two elements which combine to make an enriched picture of the object they replace. So a ship becomes a 'horse of the waves', an 'elk of the sea', a 'foam's-stallion', a 'spray-veined roller'; a battle becomes a 'sword-storm' or a 'steel-storm'; a generous earl is a 'gift-giver', a warrior is a 'crimsoner of eagles' claws', a 'reddener of wolves grins' (meaning he kills people and leaves their bodies as carrion for birds of prey and wolves). Part of a skald's skill lay in his ability to elaborate on old kennings or invent new ones. The picture is complicated by the fact that many kennings refer to gods or myths and cannot be explained without reference to those gods or myths, most of which are likely to be unknown to the general reader; the 'Odin's mead' myth which I mentioned earlier is an example. The dilemma for the translator is that if he tries to incorporate kennings, the modern reader needs copious notes to explain them; and if he simply replaces them with the word for the object they describe – 'ship' rather than 'foam's-stallion' for example – much of the poetry is lost. I have tried to catch something of each kenning, or to use some image derived from it, and sometimes I have created new ones in an effort to convey something of the vivid experience, if not always the literal sense, of Rǫgnvaldr's originals.

The exception I have made is where the kennings refer to Norse gods and myths because, as already noted, these references require too much background information to make them significant to most readers. I have usually left them out, although I have experimented in two instances by replacing Rǫgnvaldr's references to goddesses as emblems of women by substituting 'Eve' for the goddess's names, in the belief that this may be a more comprehensible way of encapsulating woman-as-myth for a modern audience.

TRANSLATING SKALDIC VERSE

Few people have published literary translations of Rǫgnvaldr's poems. Scholars who have translated the verses have agreed with the Orkney poet George MacKay Brown, who made what he called 'imitations' of some of them, that the original form is 'impossibly difficult.' Mackay Brown's imitations are exquisite, but entirely un-skaldic. The history of translating skaldic poetry in general indicates that only two or three translators have attempted to capture its full effect, with the stanzas in William Morris's saga translations of the 1870s coming closest, despite his predilection for archaisms designed to make the verses sound 'old'.

My own approach is based on the understanding that to do justice to the original, poetry must be translated into poetry which seeks equivalents for the original's sound-patterns and imaginative reach as well as its narrative sense. The *Dróttkvætt* stanza is an extreme example of poetry in which the verse-form and exaggerated language are essential to the experience the poem offers. It might be described as exoskeletal, like a crab's shell and claws: its rigid outer form shapes and defines it. At the same time its physically charged kennings and far-reaching referential scope, equivalent to the grotesque shapes and movements of a crab, give it physical presence, a sense of deeply-rooted and unique existence, as well as the potential for transformation. Attempts to convey the impact of *dróttkvætt* verses without its 'impossibly difficult' exoskeletal features is like removing a crab's shell and claws, reducing it to an unarticulated morsel of flesh which, however tasty, conveys little of the original.

Of course, attempting exact reproduction of *dróttkvætt's* effects is an ideal – in practice, no translation can be a slave to the conventions of the originals. The differences between languages, in this case the highly-inflected Old Norse language and sparsely-inflected English, make both sound-for-sound and sense-for-sense translation impossible. Poetry translation might more realistically be described as a meeting of two voices, of the minds, cultures and values each springs from, a meeting which results in a third voice, one which aims to project the best of both. Seeking equivalents for the unique sound-patterns and imaginative flair of the Old Norse originals, their exoskeletal structure and sense-rooted language are the primary means by which I have tried to ensure that the skaldic identity of Rǫgnvaldr's voice remains intact.

RǪGNVALDR

The Rǫgnvaldr revealed by his poems is somewhat different to the man portrayed in the prose of *Orkneyinga Saga*. No doubt he was, as the saga-writers' eulogy after his death puts it, 'a good friend to a great many people, lavish with money, moderate, loyal to his friends, a many-sided man and a fine poet', but his poetry reveals a more complex picture. He seems to have been able to compose in the *dróttkvætt* verse-form at will and on any subject, demonstrating how it is possible to use an apparently rigid format with casual-seeming flexibility. His most quoted poem is the first, because it is a rare listing of the skills a young aristocratic Norwegian might have been expected to acquire, as well as being brimful of the exuberance of confident youth. The next best known are the eight poems which record glimpses of his feelings, or posturings, towards the Lady Ermingerd of Narbonne, in a style that may reflect troubadour influences. Rǫgnvaldr and his men had wintered in Narbonne in the South of France on their pilgrim

sea-voyage to Jerusalem. The beautiful widow Ermingerd presided over a cosmopolitan court and
was flatteringly courted in verse by a number of
well-known troubadours. Both *Orkneyinga Saga*
and his poems describe Rǫgnvaldr's vigorous woo-
ing of her, and she is the subject of a verse competition between him and two of his fellow skald-
followers. Then there are the expected sea-poems,
descriptions of battles and sieges, the occasional
scatological squib, his delight in a friend falling
in an open sewer, and another competition with a
fellow-skald in which each composed poems on
the spot about a man in a tapestry. These are all
verses which fit the description of the intelligent
and outgoing Viking-earl the saga describes, com-
positions distinguished primarily by the opportun-
ism, wit and skill of their making.

But Rǫgnvaldr also made verses based on his
Christian beliefs, as well as a tender stanza express-
ing his grief about his wife's illness. He recorded a
range of minor incidents and confrontations which
have the sense of personal diary entries rather than
public poetry to be shared with his comrades. He
had a preoccupation with clothes, and is described
by the saga as 'something of a dandy' in his young-
er days. He composes a poem about donning a
crumpled cloak after a shipwreck, and not being
able to swagger down the gang-plank in his usual

finery. He seems irritated when describing a young woman laughing at him when he slips on the beach and he realises she has seen through the fisherman disguise he is wearing. He is annoyed when a woman called Ragna provokes him by wearing the wrong head-dress to court, a poem in which his reaction, reinforced by the saga's remark that Ragna turned Rǫgnvaldr's description of her wearing a 'mare's tail' into 'stallion's tail', takes on a highly sexualised tone. Combined with little vignettes of odd incidents – a man suddenly trying to push him over, a wet servant-girl's chattering teeth – and his frequent references to the act of making poetry, the picture emerges of an acutely observant, aware but highly self-conscious, even vulnerable, poet. The impression of the public, looked-up-to earl-poet with an inclination to look inward, is darkened by moments in some poems in which he seems to be composing entirely for himself, even talking to himself *sotto voce*, as in the poem *'Returning to Orkney he hears of faction and dissent'* (p. 41). Despite the 850 or so years which separate us, there is a strong sense of modernity in this recording of the random incidents and private thoughts of the day in verse.

Some will find words and phrases in the translations which are new to them, or not immediately comprehensible; the title of the book, for example, derived from the kenning *crimsoner of eagles' claws,* signifying 'warrior', is based on the understanding that warriors kill others and leave their corpses for birds of prey to devour. Nevertheless I have not put explanatory notes on the same page as the poems because I think it more important that the reader attends to the sounds and engages actively with the imagery, as opposed to expecting to unscramble the literal senses of each individual word on the first reading. I have listed explanations of the least obvious references and word-senses in the notes at the back of the book (p. 91), and trust that the arrangement of the poems into groups by subject matter, which follow the largely chronological sequencing of the poems as they appear in the narrative of *Orkneyinga Saga,* will also help readers orientate themselves.

I say 'readers', but of course skaldic poetry was primarily composed for oral performance; even those of Rǫgnvaldr's which are intensely personal and inward-looking seem geared towards private recitation. The translations are at their best when read out loud – declaimed in some cases, murmured in others. I hope they convey something of the skill, vigour and daring of skaldic poetry, as well as the reflective sensibility of Rǫgnvaldr's more personal verses.

Ian Crockatt

Crimsoning The Eagle's Claw

Early Poems

Tafl emk ǫrr at efla;
íþróttir kannk níu;
týnik trauðla rúnum;
tíðs mér bók ok smíðir.
Skríða kannk á skíðum;
skýtk ok rœk, svát nýtir;
hvártveggja kannk hyggja:
harpslǫtt ok bragþǫttu.

Who'll challenge my nine skills?
I'm champion at chess,
canny recalling runes,
well-read, a red-hot smith –
some say I shoot and ski
and scull skilfully too.
Best of all, I've mastered
harp-play and poetry.

Vér hǫfum vaðnar leirur
vikur fimm megingrimmar;
saurs vasa vant, es vǫrum,
viðr, í Grímsbœ miðjum.
Nús, þats mǫs of mýrar
meginkátliga lǫtum
branda elg á bylgjur
Bjǫrgynjar til dynja.

Muck, slime, mud. We waded
for five mired weeks, reeking,
silt-fouled bilge-boards souring
in Grimsby bay. Nimbly
now, our proud-prowed Bergen-
bound Sea-Elk pounds over
wave-paved auk-moors – locks horns
with foam-crests, bows booming.

30

Hér hefk hávan reistan
harðgeðjuðum varða
Dolls í døkkum helli
draug; leitak svá bauga.
Eigi veitk, hverr ýta
unnskíða ferr síðan
langa braut ok ljóta
leið of vatn it breiða.

I shape heaped-up shingle
to house thought-threats rising
from Doll's sea-dark soul-cave.
I'll dare death for treasure –
will you? Who'll – grim-purposed
wave-swimmer – launch himself
into ill-starred eel-pools,
hunt my stilled wake, quaking?

31

Sextán hefik sénar
senn ok topp í enni
jarðar elli firrðar
ormvangs saman ganga.
Þat bǫrum vér vitni,
vestr at hér sé flestar
– sjá liggr út við élum
ey – kollóttar meyjar.

I've seen them, kirk over,
apple-cheeked Eves, weave their
girl-gaggles. Girls – sixteen,
I'll swear it – isle-spinsters
with hair hacked in circles,
half-bald heads. We skaldsmen
guffaw – gales of laughter
goad them west – Shaven! Blessed!

Incidents in the Earl's Daily Life

The widow Ragna provokes him by wearing a horse-hair
scarf round her neck instead of the usual silk headwear

Aldr hefk frétt, þats feldu
fránstalls konur allar
– verðrat menja myrðir
mjúkorðr – hǫfuðdúkum.
Nú tér Hlǫkk of hnakka
haukstrindar sér binda
– skrýðisk brúðr við bræði
bengagls – merar tagli.

I've understood always –
I've spoiled them loyally
with jewelled words – wholly
believed – all Eves scarve their
hair. You, swathed-in-mares'-tails
wife, un-man your war-chief –
strong-armed, soft-mouthed gift-horse –
snide-tongued, coarsely bridled.

35

Disguised as a fisherman he spends the day helping an old Shetlander at the fishing. He is annoyed by a girl's laughter when he slips and falls on shore

---

Skelk aflar Sif silkis
svinn at umbúð minni;
hlær stórum mun meira
mær, an fallit væri.
Fár kann jarl, en árla
(ǫrlyndr) at sjá gǫrla
(hlunns drók eik af unnum
áðr) í fiskivǫðum.

Silk-tongued Eve, your scorn-wrung
witty spoof of my outfit
is dis-proportionate –
past joking, past justice.
Few'll know a noble jarl
– no 'smocked-jock fish-disher' –
hauled this oak-keeled fourern
ashore on her oar-looms.

He makes a poem about a man in a wall-hung tapestry, and challenges the skald Oddi inn litli Glúmsson to do the same, without using any of the words he used

Lætr of ǫxl, sás útar,
aldrœnn, stendr á tjaldi,
sig-Freyr Svǫlnis Vára
slíðrvǫnd ofan ríða.
Eigi mun, þótt œgir
ǫrbeiðanda reiðisk,
bríkruðr bǫðvar jǫkla
beinrangr framar ganga.

There in the frieze – frozen,
fighting Time's tight-wefted
weave – stands Old Age; rigid,
arm raised. His blade's needling
icicle-gleams shimmer
in an arrow-shower-
braving berserk's eyes. Move!
Old Bandy's still standing.

Stendr ok hyggr at hǫggva
herðilútr með sverði
bandalfr beiði-Rindi
Baldrs við dyrr á tjaldi.
Firum mun hann með hjǫrvi
hættr; nús mál, at sættisk
hlœðendr hleypískiða
hlunns, áðr geigr sé unninn.

The sea-girt, steel-kirtled
tapestry-elf stands stoop-
shouldered – sword raised boldly,
war-struck – by the door.
Men, fear his swordsmanship;
make peace now wave-racers
– keel-skis surf down rollers –
or suffer injury.

Fekk í fylkis skikkju
fangramligr ótangi;
rekkr réð hart at hnykkja
hildingi fémildum.
Sterkr vas stála Bjarki;
staka kvǫ́ðu gram nǫkkut;
afl hefr eggja skýflir
orðvandr fyr hyggjandi.

Some fool let a felon
– vice-fisted, rope-wristed –
grip your jarl's cloak, grapple
the gift-tree. Friends – swift to
save him – say he stumbled
yet stood. The madman had
brawn, not brain – our language
brawled from his mouth, gall-stained.

Liggja sék á leggjum
(láss bannar þér rásir)
kveldfǫrlustum karli
(Kúgi) járn in bjúgu.
Eiguð aldri, Kúgi,
– aptr munt settr af prettum –
– nauðrs at nýta eiða –
náttþing, ok halt sáttir.

Kugi, I see leg-irons
– unlocked you're a runner –
hobble you. Be abject –
old Fly-by-Night's slyly
conspiratorial
tryst-days – untrustworthy
snoop – are done. Stop griping,
shun loathsome oath-breakers.

Returning to Orkney he hears of faction and dissent. He counsels himself

Nú hafa gœðingar gengit
– goðfjón es þat ljóna –
– upp grafask ill rǫð greppa –
œrit mǫrg á sœri.
Þat mun þeygi sjatna
þeim, es svik viðr heima;
stígum létt á lágan
legg, meðan upp held skeggi.

Now even the noblest
need watching. Trust's breeders
embrace arch blasphemers;
even friends' oaths turn evil.
Let them fear the slow-flaring
fuse of your cautiously
stooped and lightly-stepping
stealth, while your beard's healthy.

41

Shetland Shipwreck

Brast, þás bæði lesti
– bauð hrǫnn skaða mǫnnum –
– sút fekk veðr it váta
vífum – Hjǫlp ok Fífu.
Sék, at sjá mun þykkja
snarlyndra fǫr jarla
– sveit gat vás at vísu
vinna – hǫfð at minnum.

Crack! The seams of wave-struck
ships gaped; wet, wind-wounded
crews called; 'Help' and 'Arrow'
– reef-cast, rolled – came to grief.
Words, invoke our hardships,
tell young jarls' excelling,
how – brave girls breached – each sea-
bold man – swamped, wrecked – tholed it.

Ship-wrecked, stranded at the foot of a Shetland cliff,
he contemplates her ring, plays games with his hands,
shapes poems in his head

Hengik hamri kringðan
(hanga rjúfum) tangar
(Grímnis sylg) á galga
ginnungs brúar linna.
Svá hefr glóraddar gladdan,
gagfellis, mik þella,
lóns, at leikk við mínar
lautir, hellis Gauta.

Mistle-thrush – whistle-throat –
thrill me; twill your golden
desire-inspired serpent-
ring's song round my finger.
Let the sea's soused poet
sound his voice. See, choicest
love-fare so floods me my
fingers turn tongues, singing.

Skekk hér skinnfeld hrokkinn;
skrauts mér afar lítit;
stórrs, sás stendr of órum,
stafnvǫllr, yfirhǫfnum.
Nærgis enn af úrgum
álvangs mari gǫngum
– brim rak hest við hamra
húns – skrautligar búnir.

I – salt-meadow swallowed –
strain my hide cloak vainly;
it's hardly haute couture.
Harsh shoals stopped us strolling
from high-stemmed foam-hurdlers
in silk-lined furs. The eel-plain's
surf-mares chased our chargers,
crags chafed us ragged-raw.

While he and his companions dry off round the fire he
notices Ása's teeth chattering. She'd fallen in the well.
He 'translates':

Dúsið ér, en Ása
– atatata – liggr í vatni,
– hutututu – hvar skalk sitja? –
– heldrs mér kalt – við eldinn.

"You hog the heat, leaving
Ása-sa-sa – she's a
well-soaked slave – playing shiver
music. Brrr. It's baltic."

Ala kvezk Einnarr vilja
engan Rǫgnvalds drengja
– mér kemr Gauts á góma
gjalfr – nema jarlinn sjalfan.
Veitk, at hratzk í heitum
hugþekkr firum ekki;
inn gekk, Yggs þars brunnu
eldar síð á kveldi.

All good men banned, Einnar,
except me? Expecting
gruel – my palate's pearling
with poetry – I'll show up
later. I'll not spit at –
he breaks oaths, I'm loath to
find him – his dim fire-back
where flames, like words, maim me.

The Lady Ermingerd of Narbonne

The Lady Ermingerd of Narbonne serves him drink from
a golden bowl. He takes her on his knee

Vísts, at frá berr flestu
Fróða meldrs at góðu
vel skúfaðra vífa
vǫxtr þinn, konan svinna.
Skorð lætr hár á herðar
haukvallar sér falla
– átgjǫrnum rauðk erni
ilka – gult sem silki.

Who else hoards such yellow
hair, bright lady – fair as
your milk-mild shoulders,
where milled barley-gold falls?
Chuck the cowled hawk, harry
him with sweets. Crimsoner
of eagles' claws, I covet
cool downpours of silk; yours.

Vín bar hvít in hreina
hlað-Nipt alindriptar;
sýndisk fegrð, es fundumsk,
ferðum Ermingerðar.
Nú tegask ǫld með eldi
eljunfrœkn at sœkja
– ríða snǫrp ór slíðrum
sverð – kastala ferðir.

Chaste Ermingerd hastens
to serve – the snow-curve of
her broidered brow silvered –
poured-wine beauty shining.
So swung swords gleamed – tempered
in fire's sheath, warm-flame wreathed –
when war-hardened heroes
assaulted that castle.

Still in thrall to Ermingerd, they leave Narbonne.
Rǫgnvaldr composes a verse to her, and the skalds
Ármóðr and Oddi inn litli Glúmsson follow suit

Orð skal Ermingerðar
ítr drengr muna lengi;
brúðr vill rǫkk, at ríðim
Ránheim til Jórðánar.
Enn, es aptr fara runnar
unnviggs of haf sunnan,
rístum, heim at hausti,
hvalfrón til Nerbónar.

I'll recall words – Ermingerd's –
urging heroes' surging
foam's-stallions to follow
the fluked horde to Jordan.
Don't doubt it – come autumn
home-bound sea-plunderers
– tired of south-flung mares' tails –
will track back to Narbonne.

Ek mun Ermingerði,
nema ǫnnur skǫp verði,
margr elr sorg of svinna
síðan aldri finna.
Værak sæll, ef ek svæfa,
sýn væri þat gæfa,
brúðr hefr allfagrt enni,
eina nótt hjá henni.

Ah fate, I fear you tear
my heart from Ermingerd's.
That rare man's matched with her's
must live a slave to love.
Where is beauty's lair? There
in her brow. To bed her,
just once – oh for the chance –
I crave French hive-honey.

Trautt erum vér sem ek vætti,
verðir Ermingerðar
veitk, at horsk má heita
hlaðgrund konungr sprunda,
Þvít sómir Bil bríma
bauga stalls, at ǫllu
hon lifi sæl und sólar
setri, miklu betra.

Admired Ermingerd, queen
of elegance, of all,
will you ever give way,
gift one of us a kiss?
Treasure worth ten times more
than our smitten hearts merit!
God guard you, Ermingerd,
bright girl-gold, Narbonne's sun.

In a pause in the assault on the castle he remembers previous Christmases on his friend Solmund's Norwegian estate, and compares this one favourably with them

---

Muna munk jól, þaus ólum
austr gjaldkera hraustum,
Ullr, at Egða fjǫllum,
undleygs, með Sǫlmundi.
Nú gerik enn of ǫnnur
jafnglaðr, sem vask þaðra,
sverðs at sunnanverðum
svarm kastala barmi.

I recall youth's Yuletides:
you and I – who wielded
fame-forged swords – stewarding
feasts in east-sloped Agðar.
Solmund, this southern Yuletide
– steel wound-flames leap ramparts,
cascade through the castle –
conquers all. I'm content.

There is another lull in the fighting while fires burn at the foot of the stone wall – they wait for its mortar of lime to melt. He muses

---

Unðak vel, þás vanðisk
víneik tali mínu,
– gæfr vask vǫlsku vífi
vánarlaust – á hausti.
Nú gerik enn, þvít unnum
áttgóðu vel fljóði,
– grjót verðr laust at láta
límsett – ara mettan.

Coined 'wine-oak' for woman;
wooed, all autumn taught her
hawk's tricks, Norse-talk's pleasures.
'Tell me, Mademoiselle
– wine-bruise lipped – who born of
bed boasts such pedigree?'
Lime cracks, stone falls; crimsoned
hawks claim flesh, *mon amour.*

After a skirmish with local townsfolk the warrior-poet
anticipates valour's rewards

Vǫn ák – út á Spáni
vas skjótt rekinn flótti –
– flýði margr af mœði
menlundr – konu fundar.
Því erum vér, at vǫru
væn hljóð kveðin þjóðum,
– valr tók vǫll at hylja –
verðir Ermingerðar.

I'd hoped – after scrapping
with iron-torqued foreign
pitch-forkers – blood-featured
they fled – to be united
with Ermingerd; with her –
words, scythe-bright, sang blythly,
we mowed corpse-strewn meadows –
I'd make hay, chaste lady.

Seafaring and Piracy

They anchor to ride out a storm – he remembers her
fears for him, his reassurances, their parting – as the
fleet heads south

Skalkak hryggr í hreggi,
Hlín, meðan strengr ok lína
svǫrðr fyr snekkju barði,
svalteigar, brestr eigi.
Því réðk hvítri heita
hǫskorð, es fórk norðan,
– vindr berr snart at sundi
súðmar – konu prúðri.

Wind-harrowed wave-meadows
won't cow me – our high-prowed
flood-swung longships face the
fetch – each bow-line stretches,
leather holds – I held her,
howled oaths. Now, oak-clinkered
craft – foam-tails stream aft – surf
straight for the straits; whoah!

63

Vindr hefr vǫlsku sprundi
vetrarstund frá mundum
– út berum ás at beita –
austrœnn skotit flaustum.
Verðum vér at gyrða
vánar hart fyr Spáni
– vindr rekr snart at sundi –
Sviðris við rǫ́ miðja.

Shot by gusting easterlies
from Ermingerd's embrace –
boomed sail backed, the tacking
bow heeled – the ship's reeling.
Lash that downed sail soundly
to crossed spars; storm-harried
off Spain our keel arrows –
elated – through the straits.

He finds solace in sailing and poetry after a deserter
and his companions follow the coast north. He steers a
wide curve out to sea to avoid them

Landi víkr, en leika
lǫgr tér á við fǫgrum
– síð mun seggr at hróðri
seina – norðr at einu.
Þenna rístk með þunnu
– þýtr jarðar men – barði
einum út frá Spáni
ǫfundkrók í dag hróki.

Spain's coast northward canting
– skalds can't stint on chanting –
each thrown wave's tune thrumming
through sweet-sheered strakes. Steering
an arc – keel careering
down combers, prow foaming,
spars creaking – his carping's
the cause – fathom-ringed, singing.

They attack a dromond, a North African merchant ship.
He praises Erlingr, exults in the bloodshed and victory

Erlingr gekk, þars okkur,
ógnsterkr, ruðusk merki,
frægr með fremð ok sigri
fleinlundr at drómundi.
Hlóðum vér, en víða
vas blóð numit þjóðum,
– sverð ruðu snjallir fyrðar
snǫrp – blámanna gǫrpum.

How our blood-stained standards
stream! Erlingr – extreme
in terror, blade-bristler –
bombards the doomed dromond.
Our spears cause suffering,
spread Saracen-gore. Red-
drenched blades clinch bone boldly.
We stack slain black sailors.

66

Nennum vér at vinna
– valfall má nú kalla –
(ár hefr drengr í dreyra)
drómund (roðit skjóma).
Þat mun norðr ok norðan
naddregn konan fregna
– þjóð beið ljótt af lýðum
líftjón – til Nerbónar.

The sword-storm we'd readied
– see our wound-wands feeding –
brought doom to the dromond;
death drank at that banquet.
In Narbonne Ermingerd's
ears from all points hear it –
how blade-blood cascaded,
how beasts fell to feasting.

In praise of Auðun the Red, first to board the African-crewed dromond

Gekk á drómund døkkvan
– drengr réð snart til fengjar –
upp með œrnu kappi
Auðun fyrstr inn rauði.
Þar nǫðu vér þjóðar
– því hefr aldar goð valdit –
– bolr fellr blár á þiljur –
blóði vǫpn at rjóða.

How avidly Auðun's
heart beat for fame. Claiming
all – hell-bent on bounty –
he reddened the dromond.
Christ – irresistible
His cause as the kisses
of blood-lipped blades – leads us.
Black trunks deck the soaked boards.

Jerusalem

Ek hef lagða lykkju
(leiðar þvengs) of heiði
(snotr minnisk þess svanni
sút) fyr Jórðán útan.
En hykk, at þó þykki
þangat langt at ganga
– blóð fell varmt á víðan
vǫll – heimdrǫgum ǫllum.

When snakes grieve, ice-stricken
– skalds made heath-knots, lady –
you'll wisely memorize
my lore – beyond Jordan.
We blame dim slug-a-beds
– blood's warmth reddened meadows –
scared to risk Christ's rescue,
roam far from the home-field.

71

Knút ríðum vér kauða
– kemk móðr í stað góðan –
þann í þykkum runni
þessa Lafranzmessu.

One unsound strand binding
the scrub: his land-lubber's
spine. Worn, I wend hallowed
ways. It's St. Lawrence day.

Kross hangir þul þessum
– þjóst skyli lægt – fyr brjósti,
– flykkisk fram á brekkur
ferð – en palmr meðal herða.

Christ's cross on my breast-bone.
Balm of shouldered palm-leaves
placates the poet. Ssshh!
Pilgrims crowd the hilltop.

Hvat munk yðr eða ǫðrum
ulfbrynnǫndum kynna
– heiðs lofak hilmi blíðan
háranns – nema goð sannan.

Under heaven's airy
rafters I smile, artlessly
praise our Prince. His grace is
prized first by wolves' thirst-slakers.

Sailing to Byzantium

In the town of Imbólum his friend Erlingr, the king's brother in-law, falls off a plank into an open sewer. He failed to shout 'miðhæfi' to claim right of way over townsmen coming from the opposite direction

Villat vinr minn kalla
– varð allr í drit falla –
– nær vas í því œrin
ógæfa – 'miðhæfi'.
Lítt hykk, at þá þœtti
þengils mágr, es rengðisk,
– leirr fellr grár af gauri –
góligr, í Imbólum.

Guttered were you, Erlingr?
Too gallus to rally
your wits, mouth *miðhœfi* –
muck-lover! Unlucky
almost – a king's in-law
bum's up in Imbólum's
mire! Our crown-prince clowning,
clarted in shite's motley!

They sail to Byzantium, hoping to be hired as
mercenaries in the Emperor's Varangian Guard

Ríðum Ræfils Vakri!
Rekuma plóg af akri!
Erjum úrgu barði
út at Miklagarði!
Þiggjum þengils mála!
Þokum framm í gný stála!
Rjóðum gylðis góma!
Gerum ríks konungs sóma!

Ride the spray-maned sail-horse!
Sea-ploughs don't grub field-gorse!
Bows plough the blue wave's course
to Byzantium! Norse-
men, claim that caliph's gold!
Cut through steel-storms, be bold!
Feed wolves' red grins! Withhold
wit while kings' tales are told!

Illness, Loss

Akr verðk opt fyr sjúkri
eyfitja þó sitja
– rjóð es mér in mæra
menbrík – Njǫrun síka;
heiðis fylgjask hauðri
(hauk tínik svá) mínu,
(setrs leitandi sútar
slœgr á hverju dœgri).

I brood at her bedside
– I've brought lace, necklaces,
bone combs – who lies, limbs and
lips feverish – wishing
back our glad hours hawking
low-isled water-meadows.
I shape grave words – heart-deep,
honed, brief – to imprison grief.

Eigi veitk, nær ægi
óðflýtir má knýta,
dýr es fiskiføra
feigligt, þats vér eigum.

It's said the skiff-of-meadows'
sorrow-whelmed helmsman
can't stall a wave-reined stallion,
still own what life disowns.

In Praise of Rǫgnvaldr

Hafði hollvinr lofða,
hinns mjǫð drekkr inni
sunda logs með sveigi,
sjau dœgr muni hœgri.
En ríklundaðr renndi
Rǫgnvaldr með lið skjaldat
hesti halli glæstum
hlunns at Nǫrvasundum.

The fire-gold giver's comrade's
given himself seven
daylong-contented days
carousing in the house.
Rǫgnvaldr vigorously
gallops the spray-veined stallion;
bright-painted, shields blinking,
we breach Gibraltar strait.

To the poet Ármóðr he gives a gold-inlaid spear and asks
him to make a verse in return. This is what Ármóðr says:

Eigi metr inn ítri
allvaldr gjafar skaldi
Yggs við aðra seggi
élstœrir mér fœra.
Snjallr bar glæst með gulli
grundar vǫrðr at mundum
buðlungr nýztr it bezta
blóðkerti Ármóði.

All-powerful, excelling
other lords' gift-giving
to poets – I trumpet
the storm-trampler's true worth;
our people's protector
presented – adornments
inlaid – this gold-haloed blood-
blade honed for Ármóðr's hands.

86

They lie off Crete till they get a fair wind for the Holy Land, then make Acre one Friday morning and walk ashore in such style and grandeur as is rarely to be seen in those parts. Then Þorbjǫrn svarti makes this verse:

Vask í hirð með herði
hjǫrþeys í Orkneyjum;
réð folkstara fœðir,
fyrr of vetr til styrjar.
Nú berum rǫnd með reyndum
raunsnarliga jarli
ǫrt á úrga vǫrtu
Akrsborg fríamorgin.

I was with the rouser
of war-winds in Orkney;
he'd fleshed ravens before,
fought and won that winter.
Now, his shield-rim shouldered,
the sure-footed jarl tackles
Acre's gates. It's a rain-flayed
Friday morn. We storm on.

Rǫgnvaldr Kali Kolsson
– skull-cleaver, wave-weaver –
your mind engaged with minds
before opening men's veins;
cathedral, harbour, hall
shall rehearse your verses –
skalds and skiff-men affirm
Kol's word-skilled blade-bright son.

Notes on the Translation

p. 12   *Asgard*: The gods' walled compound

p. 30   *auk-moor*: sea

        sea-elk: ship (its name in this instance)

p. 32   *Eves*: women

p. 36   *Eve*: woman

        fourern: Four-oared Shetland fishing boat

        oar-looms: The part of the oar between blade and rowlock

p. 37   *icicle-gleams*: dazzling reflections (from a sword)

p. 38   *tapestry-elf*: elf-like man woven into the tapestry

        wave-racers: warrior-seamen

        keel-skis: ships

p. 39   *gift-tree*: generous man

p. 45   *tholed*: (Icelandic *þola*, Old English *þolian*) suffered, endured stoically

p. 47   *eel-plain's surf-mares*: waves

        foam-hurdlers: ships

        salt-meadow: sea

p. 48   *shiver-music*: chattering teeth

p. 53   *milled barley-gold*: her hair

        crimsoner of eagles' claws: warrior who kills, leaving carrion for birds of prey

p. 55   *foam-stallions*: ships
        fluked horde: whales
        mares' tails: high, wind-streamed clouds
p. 58   *steel wound-flames*: swords
p. 60   *iron-torqued*: wearing iron neck-rings and / or arm-rings (compared with the Viking's gold)
p. 63   *wave-meadows*: seas
        foam-tails: wake of ships
p. 65   *fathom-ringed*: open sea all round
p. 66   *blade-bristler*: warrior
p. 67   *wound-wands*: swords
p. 71   *when snakes grieve, ice-stricken*: in winter
p. 74   *wolves' thirst-slakers*: warriors, who spill blood for wolves to drink
p. 77   *gallus* (Scots): cocky, not afraid of the consequences
        clarted (Scots): covered in
p. 78   *spray-maned sail-horse*: ship
        sea-ploughs: ships
        steel-storms: battles
        feed wolves' red grins: kill, create corpses for wolves to eat.
p. 85   *fire-gold giver*: distributor of gold that shine's like fire; generous man
p. 86   *storm-trampler*: warrior; Rǫgnvaldr
p. 87   *rouser of war-winds*: initiator of battles
        he'd fleshed ravens: he'd killed men and left their flesh to fatten ravens

Biographical Notes

IAN CROCKATT lives with his ceramic artist wife Wenna on a small croft in the North East of Scotland. He has published several collections of his own poetry, including *Flood Alert* (Chapman Publications, 1996), *Original Myths* (Cruachan Publications, 1999), *The Crucifixion Bird* (Northwords Folios, 2002), *Blizzards of the Inner Eye* (Peterloo Press, 2003), *The Lyrical Beast* (Salix Publications, 2004), and *Skald – Viking poems* (Koo Press, Aberdeen, 2009, reprinted 2011). *Original Myths*, which includes etchings by the Scottish artist Paul Fleming, was short-listed for the Saltire Society's Scottish Book of the Year Award in 2000. He has been a prize winner in a number of national literary competitions, and was awarded writer's bursaries by the Scottish Arts Council in 2004 and 2008. He has just completed a PhD thesis at Aberdeen University, focusing on the translation of Old Norse skaldic poetry.

Ian Crockatt won the prestigious 2013 Schlegel-Tieck Society of Authors Prize (for translation into English of a full-length German work of literary merit) for his translation of selected poems by Rilke, *Pure Contradiction* (Arc Publications, 2012).

Rǫgnvaldr jarl Kali Kolsson was born on his father's extensive estates in East Agðar, Norway, around 1100 – the exact year is not known. His mother inherited estates in Orkney and her brother ruled half the Orkney earldom before his martyrdom and subsequent canonisation as St. Magnús. When Kali, having adopted the name Rǫgnvaldr after a previous successful earl, assumed the earldom in 1135, he founded the cathedral at Kirkwall and dedicated it to his uncle's memory.

Rǫgnvaldr is best remembered for his building of the cathedral, for his adventurous exploits during a three year pilgrimage to Jerusalem, described in the thirteenth century *Orkneyinga Saga*, and for his magnificently skilful skaldic poetry. In 1158 he was killed in an ambush in Caithness by political opponents, and in 1192, following his own canonisation, his remains were translated to Kirkwall Cathedral.

Translator's Acknowledgements

This volume contains all thirty two of Rǫgnvaldr jarl Kali Kolsson's verses composed in the twelfth century and preserved in the compilation of (mostly) medieval manuscripts which make up *Orkneyinga Saga*. I have also included several verses by other *skálds* [poets] who were part of Rǫgnvaldr's entourage, and the three other verses attributed to Rǫgnvaldr which are found in different manuscript sources.

The Old Norse versions printed here are taken from the latest edition of Rǫgnvaldr's poems, which are part of the international on-line Skaldic Project (abdn.ac.uk/skaldic) which aims to edit, translate and make available the entire corpus of 5000 or more extant Old Norse skaldic verses. The project is also producing the edition in book form under the generic title *Skaldic Poetry of the Scandinavian Middle Ages*. The thirty two of Rǫgnvaldr's verses from *Orkneyinga Saga*, as well as those of Oddi inn litli Glúmsson and Ármóðr reproduced here, appear in Volume II Part 2 edited by Professor Judith Jesch. Volume ll, which has the title *Poetry from the kings*, is edited overall by Professor Kari Ellen Gade and I am grateful to both for permission to reproduce the Old Norse poems. The three verses preserved in different documents have yet to be published in the Skaldic Project edition, but are reproduced here in versions also edited by Judith Jesch. I am grateful to her and to Kari Ellen Gade for allowing me to use them too.

All English language prose quotations from *Orkneyinga Saga* (pp. 20, 21 and 87) are from the 1968 Penguin Classics translation by Hermann Pálsson and Paul Edwards.

Many people played a part in the making of this book; particular thanks to Wayne, Tarrin, Karen, Lisa (downstairs), Lisa (upstairs) and Declan for theirs. Special thanks to Wenna for her love and support, as well as for the atmospheric images which enliven these pages.

Thanks also to all who attended the Cambridge University Kenning Symposium in July 2011 and gave me the confidence to keep translating, and to everyone at the Centre for Scandinavian Studies, University of Aberdeen, who put up with my over-enthusiasm for skaldic poetry: *skol*!

No-one could work on these poems without being aware of the huge contribution made to our understanding of them and their context by many scholars, in recent years by Judith Jesch and Paul Bibire in particular.

Anyone wanting to discover the secrets of how skaldic poetry achieves its effects should read Roberta Frank's 1978 book *Old Norse Court Poetry: The* Dróttkvætt *Stanza*, which brings alive its skills and transformative beauty like no other.

Versions of some of these translations were first published in *New Writing Scotland*, *Northwords Now* and *Octavius*.

Also available in the series
ARC CLASSICS: NEW TRANSLATIONS OF
GREAT POETS OF THE PAST
Series Editor: Jean Boase-Beier

FRANCO FORTINI
Poems
Translated from the Italian by Michael Hamburger

MARCELIJUS MARTINAITIS
The Ballads of Kukutis
Translated from the Lithuanian and introduced
by Laima Vince

VLADIMIR MAYAKOVSKY
Pro Eto – That's What
Translated from the Russian by Larisa Gureyeva
& George Hyde and introduced by John Wakeman
Complete with 11 photomontages by
Alexander Rodchenko, reproduced in colour.

ED. PETER ORAM
The Page and The Fire
POEMS BY RUSSIAN POETS ON RUSSIAN POETS
Selected, translated from the Russian
and introduced by Peter Oram

SALVATORE QUASIMODO
The Night Fountain: Selected Early Poems
Translated from the Italian
by Marco Sonzogni & Gerald Dawe

GEORG TRAKL
To the Silenced: Selected Poems
Translated from the German and introduced by Will Stone

RAINER MARIA RILKE
Pure Contradiction: Selected Poems
Translated from the German and introduced by Ian Crockatt

EMILE VERHAEREN
Selected Poems
Translated from the French and introduced by Will Stone

ROSE AUSLÄNDER
While I am Drawing Breath
Translated from the German
by Jean Boase-Beier and Anthony Vivis

Further titles of poetry in translation are available in
'Arc Visible Poets', 'Arc Translations', 'Arc Anthologies' and
'New Voices from Europe & Beyond' (anthologies)

www.arcpublications.co.uk